FORBEARANCE

The Poiema Poetry Series

Poems are windows into worlds; windows into beauty, goodness, and truth; windows into understandings that won't twist themselves into tidy dogmatic statements; windows into experiences. We can do more than merely peer into such windows; with a little effort we can fling open the casements, and leap over the sills into the heart of these worlds. We are also led into familiar places of hurt, confusion, and disappointment, but we arrive in the poet's company. Poetry is a partnership between poet and reader, seeking together to gain something of value—to get at something important.

Ephesians 2:10 says, "We are God's workmanship..." *poiema* in Greek—the thing that has been made, the masterpiece, the poem. The Poiema Poetry Series presents the work of gifted poets who take Christian faith seriously, and demonstrate in whose image we have been made through their creativity and craftsmanship.

These poets are recent participants in the ancient tradition of David, Asaph, Isaiah, and John the Revelator. The thread can be followed through the centuries—through the diverse poetic visions of Dante, Bernard of Clairvaux, Donne, Herbert, Milton, Hopkins, Eliot, R. S. Thomas, and Denise Levertov—down to the poet whose work is in your hand. With the selection of this volume you are entering this enduring tradition, and as a reader contributing to it.

—D.S. Martin
Series Editor

FORBEARANCE

Poems

CAMERON BROOKS

CASCADE *Books* • Eugene, Oregon

FORBEARANCE
Poems

Poiema Poetry Series

Copyright © 2025 Cameron Brooks. All rights reserved. Except for brief quotations in critical publications or reviews, no part of this book may be reproduced in any manner without prior written permission from the publisher. Write: Permissions, Wipf and Stock Publishers, 199 W. 8th Ave., Suite 3, Eugene, OR 97401.

Cascade Books
An Imprint of Wipf and Stock Publishers
199 W. 8th Ave., Suite 3
Eugene, OR 97401

www.wipfandstock.com

PAPERBACK ISBN: 979-8-3852-3285-7
HARDCOVER ISBN: 979-8-3852-3286-4
EBOOK ISBN: 979-8-3852-3287-1

Cataloguing-in-Publication data:

Names: Brooks, Cameron.

Title: Forbearance : Poems / Cameron Brooks.

Description: Eugene, OR: Cascade Books, 2025 | Poiema Poetry Series

Identifiers: ISBN 979-8-3852-3285-7 (paperback) | ISBN 979-8-3852-3286-4 (hardcover) | ISBN 979-8-3852-3287-1 (ebook)

Subjects: LCSH: Poetry. | American poetry.

Classification: PS3625 B76 2025 (print) | PS3625 (ebook)

for Jenny & Rudy

He didnt think the horse would quit him but he was sure the horse had thought about it.

—Cormac McCarthy, *The Crossing*

Contents

I

Chore 3
McKennan's Golden Hour 4
Prairie Archipelago 5
The Mower and the Nun 6
Blessed Zephyr 7
A More Capacious Phrase 8
The Cottonwoods Were Sowing Starry Seeds 9
Gravity 10
Once Again, the Orchard 11
The Seagull Scans a Fallow Field 12
East River, South Dakota 13
Driving at Night 15
Red Light 16
Death of a Piano 17
Ahmad Jamal Lives 18
The Barista 19
Early Morning Embers 20
Forbearance 22
Ponderosa 23
Antique Store, Somewhere, South Dakota 25
The Centurion 26
Icarus Flashback 27
Poem from the Future 28
The Average Lifespan of a Rabbit 29
Post-blizzard 30
Prayer at Puget Sound 31

Contents

II

Coming to Terms 35
Off Silence 36
On Silence 37
White Space 38
Privatio Boni 39
When the Black Hills Are White 40
Pickup Smells 41
Spring & Disbelief 42
Efficient Poem 43
Nepsis 45
To a Church Coat Rack 46
The End of Confession 47
Time-tampering 48
The Handyman's Son 50
My Father's Thighs 52
Turning Point 53
Moses Grows Weary 54
Macrina's Thread 56
North Shore Vesper 57
Pactola 58
Telemachus 59
Surfeit 60
Sea Change, Big Sur 62
Beach Towel with Pizza Box 63
The Problem of Walgreens 64
D.B.M. 65
William Shows Up 66
Amarillo Sepia 67
Moonhand 68
Aubade 69
Nocturne 70
Camp Judson 71
Three Ways of Looking at Spearfish 72
Late Aspiration 76

Acknowledgments 77

I

Chore

Let the greased teeth of the chainsaw
        saw through an ash log's
                still-green flesh,

its spat-back chips
        splintering your sweaty shins;
                let lactic acid lacerate

the lariat cordage of your arms,
        your turgid, pulsing palms,

until some one might find
        in the runaway chore of your life
            an anvil

        from which to draw a sword.

McKennan's Golden Hour

In the garden in the middle of the park
in the middle of town, we were lying
in the grass one evening. Must've been

the very end of August because
every burr oak, ash, and magnolia
seemed somehow greener than ever

and younger. We were lying in the grass,
as I say, waiting for others to arrive
and fretting about the coming weeks

which are by now many weeks gone by.
And given it was evening, light spun
through the sprightly trees and all over

the quartzite path leading to the stone
flower fountain in the middle
of the garden, where we were lying

in the grass. Yet it never occurred
to me to lift you by the hand to see
what everlasting thing might be found

in the middle of the fountain, till now.

Prairie Archipelago

They say some ancient glacier is to blame
for this—a flooded farmhouse, a gaunt silo
rising from a nameless lake. We drift by

in silence, casting our lines around the rubble,
permitting the wind to carry us where it carries
all things: whitecaps and walleye, three pelicans

squatting at shore beside a shot tractor tire.
Why have we come here? To fish, of course,
and to savor the contingency of being

between bites; to wait, wondering at the old
highway that plunges into the lake; to watch
thick thunderheads descending from the north.

The Mower and the Nun

The man who mows the ditch
between the strips of interstate
found it worthwhile to leave us
patches of wild sunflowers
every several miles.
Even at eighty-per-hour
you can't miss 'em: sunny thumbprints
pressed against the paper
bag browns of late September.
I will never thank him.

And I will never thank the nun
I saw watering her brittle yard
with a hose—in full garb!
That strange religious habit
of the celibate salt of this dearth.
Doesn't she know October
is coming and November is coming
and December comes only to steal
and kill and destroy? She knows
life, life abundantly.

Blessed Zephyr

Spirit, breath, wind
surging in multitudes
of ripe sunflowers
like electricity

lifting blackbird
and raptor and
the damp coal nose
of a buck.

Laughter cracks
the face of the deep
lake (tongue-inflated-cheek)
and every last

stalk, shuck, and kernel
rattles like a holy
plaything.
Never inert

because never deserted
to that quietude
tantamount to
oblivion.

A More Capacious Phrase

Suppose there are no perfect synonyms,

                        so that to call a spade a *spade* is not

to say a *scoop* or *shovel*, but every word

                        is what it is and not some other word

dressed up in different letters. A hummingbird

                        might lazily be described as *pink* and *green*

(a truth so small it feels more like a lie).

                        But if, unsatisfied, we turn to our

thesaurus for a more capacious phrase,

                        we find there not a ready-made supply

of substitutes for pink and green, but words

                        whose purchase on a hummingbird obtain

to disparate degrees and (here's the rub)

                        not one of them cut out for just this task.

The Cottonwoods Were Sowing Starry Seeds

The cottonwoods were sowing starry seeds
across the yard, summer's feather-gravity
arranging their orbits around the garden
shed and peonies and pear trees.

She strolled through constellations
in that gilded hemisphere, adorned
in a linen dress the color of her
skin, the color of sheer light

tilting through crowns of cottonwoods
and coruscating in the evening
wind, in the solar systems
drifting between her
fingertips.

Gravity

Rounding a corner en
route to the orchard,
a sudden clearing gives way
to infinite convexed sky,
not unlike the ocean seen
from a great height, so great

you almost perceive
earth's curvature warp-
ing spacetime. Later I can

hardly believe how clusters
of ripe red-gold apples dangle
from their branches, the ease
with which September
stems yield even
to the sticky
fingers of

a child, lifted through
the leaves to grasp what
seems to him the sweetest,
most attractive sphere of all.

Once Again, the Orchard

Once again, the orchard aches
beneath the fragile weight of October
and the ooze of too-ripe apples beneath boots.
You may surely eat of every tree—only
beware the hidden worm and the wasp,
the sting that is the bitterness of the first bite.
Wasn't it sweeter last time?

When half the sky explodes in starlight
while the other submits to shadows and clouds
and a lashing of heat lightning—
then all is clear. You hear the silence
you were anxious to hear
in the warm breeze above the valley before the storm.
You are nothing before the storm.

Embellished images line the walls
of the corridors of memory.
Echoes of seasons blurred with seasons
passing. Anticipation budding
in liminality. The promise of the apple
blossom; a dim scent of rain. Longing
after longing and longing again.

The Seagull Scans a Fallow Field

The seagull scans
a fallow field
in search of God

knows what.
Have you lost your way,
mistaking this God

forsaken wilderness
for the shores you were
created for? Perhaps

you were gulled
by the Prairie
waves into believing

you'd discovered country
good for more than
flying over, maybe

even a place
to stay. It's okay,
so did we.

East River, South Dakota

I

Our Desert Fathers and Mothers deserted Rome
to pray and work in the wild, *ora et labora*.
Anthony the Great, Moses the Black,
Macrina the Younger, all hungry for hunger,

solitude and silence, austerity and thirst,
sweet nectar of the desert's prickly pear
and a life leashed and liberated by that
solitary Rule, *ora et labora*, pray and work.

II

Of course, even St. Anthony was plagued
by temptations, dens of nasty demons,
bright silver platters, and, I imagine,
by rumors of Rome. But the burning

and the yearning, was that not the goal?
Not the nectar so much as the prick
of the pear; nor salvation from the desert
heat, but yielding to its refining fire.

III

Arcane waters fashioned these High Plains
and deserted us to the fires by which we must
learn to live and move and have our longings
shaped by the vagaries of weather

and the vicissitudes of prayer and violet
August skies alight with stars and burning
stars and the deathless wash of wind
upon this oceanic plain.

Driving at Night

Out here, the horizon has sunk
to the humble reaches of headlights,

which bore through boundless darkness
the way a fish darts through its lake
(straight on, heedless of all other lakes)

or the way a spaceship slips through
time, so quiet. Out here, the sky
has swallowed the prairie entire,

the lamps of distant barns like stars
from forgotten constellations, guiding us

home and so far from home. How strange
it feels to travel at the speed of light.

Red Light

Stuck in traffic again
long enough to remember
we're hurtling
around a flaming star
at sixty-seven thousand
miles per hour in a galaxy
of one to four hundred
billion stars in a universe
of two trillion galaxies
in the mind of God.

Someone is blaring
blink-182 behind me.
And the man in the car
ahead stretches and slides
his right hand beneath his wife's hair
to caress the curve of her neck.
She's looking out the window,
watching a jogger and
a golden retriever go by.
The light turns green,
cars resume their honking,
and I have never felt less alone.

Death of a Piano

In the end, his piano
playing drove her mad,
drove her to drive her car
through the back wall
of the garage and into his
precious baby grand
on the other side.
He wasn't playing at the time
(though he might as well
have been) when taut steel
strings began to fray and snap,
flower pots and chunks
of drywall crumbling
all over the keys
in some discordant dirge
of an oath forsaken
many nocturnes ago.

Ahmad Jamal Lives

Upon discovering the great jazz pianist was still alive in June of 2022.

Was it your radiant idiom that led me
to assume you had gone out
with the last true titans of jazz?
Such protean hands: twin shadows hovering
over the face of the keys,
rising to the level of mythology, then
striking both ivories and ebonies
in such chords and discords
as have scarcely been conceived
since the epoch of Thelonious Monk.
Ruby, my dear, perhaps that Spirit
who wrought the world works anew
each age, each day, each flaming
flower of the Poinciana, and this day
on which Ahmad Jamal lives.

The Barista

It started out how most obsessions do:
without intent or purpose. He only knew
he liked to hang around cafe hipsters,
intrigued at how they traded tasting notes.
He took a shift, learned to pull espresso
and speak of it in scientific terms,
terms like *extract* and *refractometer*.
His palate grew impressively refined,
his tongue more like a scanner than a tongue.
He could articulate exactly why
he did not like all that he did not like
(and why, of course, you shouldn't either).
Even his hipster friends got reticent
where coffee was concerned, afraid to sound
uncouth, unlearned. Some took to tea.
Eventually it seemed the more he drank
the less he'd tolerate imperfect brews.
So less and less he drank, until one day
all coffee seemed derivative of his
quixotic taste. Caffeine pills took its place.

Early Morning Embers

Your cigarette glowed like the last dying star
of some frigid galaxy as you stood exhaling fog
and smoke before dawn. When summer came,

you would sit on your step and smoke and yell
on the phone with your mother in your Long Island
accent. That was when we shared a backyard.

At first I planted three magnolias—hoping you
wouldn't read between the lines. Magnolias are
patient trees, though, and you needed nicotine.

So I tried a wooden panel fence, asking for your
permission this time: *Sure,* you said, *a little privacy
can't hurt.* In the morning I found all three trees

flattened under the fence, which had blown over
in the night. I put it up again, more deliberately.
And once I was reading while you were smoking

on your step. Somehow you saw me—you saw me
and tossed a bag of fresh baked cookies over
the fence, as if to heap burning coals over my head.

We had to stand ten feet apart so you could see
my face when I thanked you, ashamed. It was
winter again by the time I realized you were

gone. No more early-morning embers, no coughing or yelling or baked goods. Just a useless fence and three lopsided magnolias shivering in the snow.

Forbearance

Wind—unlike the likely droughts
and stubbled summer lawn,

or the cicada's tymbal cry;
unlike the absolute emptiness

of fields under snow at night
with their highways like blue stitches;

unlike the austere Cooper's hawks
perched upon fence posts

and splintered billboards—wind
was the one thing she refused

to abide: how it lashes the prairie,
the porch swing, the sky, penetrating

the slightest cracks of her
worn house, her worn face.

Ponderosa

> *What livelihood can repay a human creature for a life*
> *spent in this huge sameness?*
> *—Robert Louis Stevenson*

Dizzied by swells of prairie grass,
        a huge sameness, a vast
expanse of oceanic green;

irked, too, by retro billboard ads
        along the interstate
(meant less to sell than, well, divert

one's gaze from the vertiginous
        vistas of sprawling plain),
I wind up here again, walking

deep rings of ponderosa pine.
        Boughs jeweled in April ice
they circle a marble reservoir,

stand sentinel atop steep crags
        to curb infinity.
I listen for the snow-silence

and picture old sailors who saw
        in their delirium
endless green meadows in lieu

of endless seas, longing to hurl
        themselves overboard.
What relief they must have felt,

once moored, to find the earth once more
        a fixed, familiar place,
of trees and stones and clock towers.

Antique Store, Somewhere, South Dakota

A fading portrait of a stoic tribal chieftain
in his feathered headdress, sitting a horse.
A corner for a shoddy chestnut saddle
and other equestrian tack: leather boots,
ten pair, a bucket of spurs, thin lariats
strung around the pommel. Wide-brim hats,
of course, with beaded drawstrings for riding
in the wind. Reams of vintage postcards:
Mt. Rushmore, Fort Collins, St. Paul.
Next, stacks of rusty license plates for every
state west of Missouri. Ten dollars each.
Glass cases of curios: phantom keys,
pocket knives, Zippo lighters, dead
wrist watches, other nameless trinkets.
Embroidered dish towels, Larimar jewelry.
Spoons. Magazine clippings of slim house-
wives tilted in their aprons, advertising
kitchenware. A colossal bison head
trophy-mount, protruding from the wall.
Racks of double-barrel rifles and crimson
Navajo print rugs and hundreds of
growlers, bottles, jars, cans, and mugs.
One glossy green ashtray from Vegas.
Some cowboy poetry. Way in the back,
with a red sale sticker, a woodcut profile of
Jesus, beard gathering dust; cheap gods don't sell.

The Centurion

—Matthew 8:5

Such signal devotion
to this suffering servant

(and doubtless one of many)
to go out, as we say, on a limb

like that—that act
ingredient of all *bona fide*

belief, to hope without
presumption that it will be

done as one has believed.
But say the word, he said,

and it will be so. So, marveling,
Christ said to him: *Go*

Icarus Flashback

Too hot to sleep, too late
to think
straight, I sat up in bed,
tore my t-shirt

from my damp chest
and tossed it across the room

when it became a crackling
comet of sparks, arcing
through the darkness

for one radiant instant

(the way he might have
remembered things)
before crashing

to the carpet. Mute.

And I thought, for all
the brilliant ways
to squander one's odds,

it might yet be possible
not to.

Poem from the Future

—for Ted

Perhaps it was only the slip
of a single keystroke that dated
your letter a year from now,
the one with the poem
you wrote that morning
about a cluster of gaunt trees,
bone white, holding ballet positions
along the bank of a black lake.

I prefer to believe, however,
that you've written me from the future,
that a year from now you'll still be
rising each morning
to bear witness to a blue heron

in your rear-view mirror,
gliding in low over the lake,
breaking the water's sheen
with the tips of its wings.

The Average Lifespan of a Rabbit

The average lifespan of a rabbit is
        about eleven months, at least for those
                prolific cottontails who populate

my neighborhood along their only ride
        around the sun: one summer surfeited
                on clover, grass, and dandelion greens,

one winter scraping by on frozen bark
        beneath great drifts of ice. A lucky few
                will live to see a season twice, the thaw

of spring, perhaps, and in a blossom-breeze
        recall the earliest days of rabbit youth,
                the unlikely circle of their fickle
                        lives just setting out across the earth.

Post-blizzard

I

A haggard rabbit sits in the shadows of the eaves
of the house, looking out at the snowbound yard
with its marble eye and wondering what we're all
wondering: *how am I supposed to get through this?*

Up the street someone has revved a snow blower
and begun chugging down the sidewalk in the dark,
a headlight like that of a locomotive emerging
from a tunnel, its plume of smoke thrown snow.

II

For a while the world contracts, and we content
ourselves within it. Soon the rabbits will burrow
to the fence and back, while the rest of the yard
forgets. Anyway, who wouldn't prefer one sure
path to the many we entertain but cannot take?

Prayer at Puget Sound

Countenance this leaden dawn
on which even Olympus sulks

beyond the winded Sound,
and every gull seems desperate

for some arm to perch upon.
You saw me yesterday, right

here, edge of the bluff, singing
in the zenith sun with the eagles

who know your name. Already
I'm forgetting the Sound,

already rewriting these words.
Countenance this leaden dawn.

Break golden over mountains.
Wreathe my heavy crown with light.

II

Coming to Terms

The Poet only had so much to say
        till he set out to say more than he knew,
the textbook definition of a fool,

it's true, yet this he likewise realized
        was not far from the point: to reach for words
and into words whose latitudes can't but

betray the sheer enormity of *things*.
        Yes, words of scandalous particularity,
like tokens of an order infinite

as stars. When God told Abraham to count them—
        this was no lesson in arithmetic.
The deathless promise is what shook the old

man's heart, a vision like a fisher's net
        cast wide across the desert sky, cool night-
winds crooning in a tamarisk, the thought

that from a distant time or point of view,
        even these constellations might prove a speck
in some still greater harmony of stars.

Off Silence

Hip mystics tell me silence is the salve
        for a disintegrated soul, a sort
                of detox from that stupefying din

called postmodernity, even a *sine*
        qua non for making out the quiet Voice
                within. Perhaps. As yet, I still enjoy

a bit of bebop while I do the dishes,
        the shining saxophone of Lester Young
                spinning in my living room. Or, stuck

in traffic on a gloomy day, I'd rather
        put on something cool by Clifford Brown
                to pass the time, a trinity of brass

and bass and ride converging with the verve
        of fathomless potentialities
                becoming what they only could become.

On Silence

Dishes done, both sides of a record spun,
      stylus skating silently along
           its runout groove as gusts of snow outside

snuff out the lastlight of another day.
      Another day comes down to this: my sense
           that silence never proved an emptiness.

White Space

Awake to snow-freighted pines,
    blue snow upon the pasture

where five shining horses graze
    with snow in their manes. They

know grass has begun to grow
    beneath the snow, having tasted

it only yesterday. A bruised bouquet
    of dried chili peppers dangles

from the doorframe of my cabin
    like a frozen claw. Crescent moons

of snow slouch in the nose slits
    and eye sockets of a deer skull

pegged to a post—its antlers
    and remaining teeth so dull

against unadulterated drifts
    of snow, not white, not ivory,

just bone, the hollow color of bone.

Privatio Boni

We cast creepy shadows on the living room wall,
provoking the cats. They squat in an amber puddle
of evening sun, heads cocked at forty-five degrees
like novice philosophers who haven't yet grasped

what Thomas Aquinas meant in *Summa Theologica*
part one, question forty-eight, article one—namely,
that, as we know darkness by light's absence, so too,
evil is a privation of the Good, essentially a shadow

of being. Our cats do not care much for philosophy.
They pay no mind to the puppeteers performing
strange arts behind them, nor the late-August light
tilting through windows and philodendron fronds.

They could not be convinced, for instance, that
such shadows, though *privatio*, don't really exist,
and won't without warning pounce from the wall
like a pair of wolves—baring their actual fangs!

When the Black Hills Are White

with snow, it's like lumbering
Paul Bunyan has dropped a whole box

of matches on a powdered-sugared
birthday cake for Babe

the ox, just as he was reaching
to light its evergreen candles.

Pickup Smells

The strongest scent's a final sip of Coke
mixed in its can with spat tobacco juice,
Dad's musky leather Carhartts on the dash,
the cab's upholstery, ripe with coffee stains,
dog fur, and dust sputtered through broken vents.
In early spring, or on some winter day
that smacks of early spring, the floor mats shed
their ice and waft about the cab bootprints
tracked in since October or so: of pine,
alfalfa, milkweed, smoke, and cow manure,
of rust and gas and blood from last year's stag,
the one we hauled across a jagged field
in fall's last incandescent blush, his neck
so adamant, so warm against my touch
as I knelt down beside the truck to pose
for a picture, the sweet metallic bite
of blood, of death, of life leaving the earth.

Spring & Disbelief

The blackened rags of snow have finally fled,
      and rivers ramify the fields
           like leaden veins.

A shelter belt of rawboned brush reveals
      spring's latest scars, pale plastic bags
           like bandages

wound haplessly around denuded limbs,
      stripped bare of bark by cottontails
           eons ago.

Thin shafts of cloud dissolve to slate blue sky,
      the noonday sun a white-hot coin.
           Phantom-like,

the park swing sways in a vaguely-floral breeze.
      Reach out your hand, it says, *embrace*
           this wounded place.

Efficient Poem

Tearing across I-90
at exactly eighty-two,
cruise control,
sunset

torching the back
of my skull,
this uncanny prairie
all awash in firelight

again. I'm listening
to an episode on
the decline of the West,
more or less, and considering

purchasing a copy
of Jacques Ellul's
The Technological Society

from the Internet
with my Smartphone
in my right hand;
in my left hand,
the leather steering wheel
of a black sedan.

Outside, stoic raptors perch
on tattered billboards
promoting goods
whose utility seems
alien to me or
any living thing.

Nepsis

O, how to guard the nexus of the heart
with so much Netflix to devour!

To a Church Coat Rack

Wheeled out from the shadows
of your usual solitude,

you unassumingly assume
position in the narthex hallway,

arms outstretched like a scarecrow
crucifix. No respecter of persons,

you offer ample hangers
to young and old, short and tall,

tweed overcoats and windbreakers both.
Soon you will exude the awkward

aroma of one hundred closets,
perfumes and body odors,

having borne outside
the sanctuary the raiments

of another winter, that we might
let loose our thawing praise.

The End of Confession

I never reach the bottom
of my list of weekly sins

before a pardon interrupts
my penitence. Rending my

garments, I begin: *Father,
I have sinned against heaven*

and before you! But then,
a robe, a ring—new shoes.

Time-tampering

I

We circle the bonfire like statues,
faces flashing. *If you could rewind
your life*, someone asks, *start over
from any moment, how far back
would you go?*
                      A stone's throw west,
the Strait of Juan de Fuca courses
toward its Pacific rim, vast and black
and salted with pale constellations.

Children of the 90s, we've seen
Back to the Future, know the perils
of time-tampering, how any false step
could trouble one's maternal relations,
or worse. But what might be reversed?
Misplaced pocket-knives. Tenth-grade
physics class. Ghastly solecisms . . .

II

A tug boat is hauling a ponderous barge
across the deep strait, both vessels
progressing at an equal pace,
the distance between them fixed
by some unseen towline.

When the fire's last embers give to
smoldering, everything goes
moonlight-mute except the sound
washing over soft shore-stones.
And I wonder how many hours
until sunrise, and suddenly I can
think of nothing but the inevitability
of that sunrise and perhaps another
day, another chance, another life.

The Handyman's Son

For weeks after he changed
        the bathroom light fixture,
he found himself unsure
        whether he got it right,

fastened the wire nuts tight
        enough. *It's like to like—*
black to black, white
        to white—right? He flips

the switch; the bulb flits on.
        That's good. But still he fears
something is off, or loose,
        or otherwise unsound.

He lies awake at night,
        imagining his wife
helpless in the shower
        some hour he's away

as, up in the attic
        the wires emit a spark
that kindles into flame,
        and—just like that—his house

is burning to the ground.
        He pictures her calling
for help in a bathrobe,
        from the neighbor's front yard

and later, the disappointment
        on her face when he
pulls up, too late, to find
        her sitting on the curb

beside a strikingly
        good-looking fireman,
his jacket draped over
        her shoulders, his thermos cup
steaming in her hands.

My Father's Thighs

—2 Chronicles 10–12

When I became the king of Israel
    the people grumbled, as they often do.
They claimed my father, Solomon, was harsh
    and overburdened them with heavy yokes.

They wanted me to cut them slack. I sought
    my father's (senile) elders for advice.
And, wiping spittle from their beards, they said,
    you give them what they want, a lighter load.

My buddies saw things otherwise. One night
    around a jar we found a clever comeback
to the people's cries. *You've had enough?*
    My member's thicker than my father's thighs!

In retrospect, I might have used a softer
    turn of phrase. The Hebrews did not take
to heavier taxes or longer days ... And
    they stoned to death the taskmaster I sent.

Shortly after this the kingdom tore
    in two. Shishak king of Egypt plundered
Jerusalem, marauding the temple stores,
    my father's shields of gold, which I replaced
    with shields of bronze—all I could afford.

Turning Point

I knew you passed me the pickle jar
not to test my grip
so much as to finally admit

yours was failing, and had been for some time.
That all the pickles, olives, and jars of
salsa, carrots and apple sauce,

sealed down in the dark
cellar would go to waste, unless
someone took the torch down

there and did something about it.

Moses Grows Weary

Let's suppose the worst
lies behind us—

the serpents, the blood,
the flight beneath the sea—

such that all that
remains is the only thing

ever truly asked of us:
to keep still

in every desert interval
and the long ellipses between

mountains, to be borne
again on the backs of eagles.

Even then: stillness
strains the soul

and body both, and
the staff of God weighs heavily

after all this time,
this burning hillside.

Hold up my arms, my
brothers, hold up my wearied arms.

And together we will watch
the bruised Sun sink

into the earth, victorious.

Macrina's Thread

From her deathbed
    she cheered

her tearful brother.
    Do not despair!

she said, that death
    unravels the body

like a spool of thread,
    the body you've grown

to love. In time
    we'll be re-spun,

every one woven
    into a tapestry

brilliant and far
    more beautiful

than you've supposed,
    yet verily, verily
       you.

North Shore Vesper

—Duluth, Minnesota

I'll meet you at the bottom of the lake.
We'll watch our friends and enemies ripple
the effervescent sky—then perforate

the firmament like wished-upon nickels
flicked into a fountain and flashing while
they fall. All skipping stones will fall: triples

and fours and fives, gathered to the fertile
garden of rock at the base of the lake,
a congregation waiting for the sky

to part, to feel the sunshine on their faces,
to feel the sun shine on their craggy faces.

Pactola

When all the gold was thought   to have been shaken out
of these old pine-black hills,   they ripped a reservoir
to flood the vacant mining   town of Pactola.

Now glossy motor boats   wrinkle the lake's blue face
all summer long, as schools   of rainbow trout shimmer
in shallows effervescent   with summer sun.

But once, at dawn, when fog   weighed heavy on the pines
I watched a scuba diver   rise out of the lake—
as from a mythic scene—   with flaming in his fist.

Telemachus

     —after Homer's Odyssey

Of his resemblance to his shipwrecked father
he would hear no end. His ruddy complexion

and the shape of his head, the not-yet-calloused
hands and feet. For Helen, it was the salt-cut

expression of his eyes, as that of a man
accustomed to supplicating some furious sea.

Above all, how he sailed a crew to Pylos
for so much as a rumor of one thought dead,

then flew on chariots through the far country
to Sparta, taking nothing for a guide save

the footfalls of a god and the lion in his chest.

Surfeit

Wave after wave after frothy wave:

                        unremitting, unnecessary.

A surfeit of salty surf—

                        of seaweed, shells, and other flotsam

tossed to shore, to wharf, tossed

                        toward nothing and nowhere at

all. The gratuitous tides of tanned faces

                        steaming along sidewalks. A kid

with a shaggy hairdo racing barefoot

                        and a pale surfboard beneath his arm.

He barely catches the bus home.

                        (In a way, he is all of us.)

Seated behind that kid with sand

                        in his sandy hair, we watch

out the windows as this hazy beach

                                      town passes in a red incandescence

I have seen a thousand times before

                                      and have not seen in all my life.

Sea Change, Big Sur

Now that you exist
        like no thing ever did,
ridiculous the thought:
        we do, but needn't.

The sea, obsidian
        beneath a cloak of fog;
time-blackened rock
        its interlocutor.

From the cove, the sea's
        a pale sea-green.
(And not for want of words.)
        Waves bifurcate on rock.

And higher up the cliff,
        the lusty sun stretches
and sets out for a jog
        over the turquoise sea,

as all along the shore
        for periphrastic miles
stretch petals red and gold
        superfluously.

Beach Towel with Pizza Box

We agree it would be nice if your legs
always looked that way, and my abs,

lustrous and flat in the salted light,
as I emerge from the surf and return
to you on shore for yet another slice.

In this life, we'd be king and queen
of Bradley Beach, Del Ponte's pizza

delivery dude our personal valet.
And your ethereal thigh-gapped legs
would forever shine in the light of a sun

that neither rises nor fades, and together
we'd be beautiful, immutable, afraid.

The Problem of Walgreens

The woman at the front of the checkout line
thrust her finger at the man behind the counter.
Apparently half her groceries had been mispriced
and she could not afford that. *I'm sorry but*

there's nothing I can do, the man said. *Who
is responsible?* she demanded. *Who is responsible
for this?* And (if you can believe it) he said
Corporate is. The frozen pizza on the counter

began to sweat. *Is there a phone number
I can call? I would like to speak with someone
about this.* There was no such number. Again
he said he was very sorry but there was nothing

he could do. So she threw her hands in the
air, like swatting at flies, muttered a curse
and stormed off, catching her step for a split
second before the sliding door's indifferent
yawn, then vanished behind a curtain of rain.

D.B.M.

Donor Breast Milk. You weren't expecting that?
Makes two of us. Nor was I expecting
the routine buzz of a hand sanitizer dispenser
outside our stuffy N.I.C.U. room to verge
on the liturgical, those early, swollen hours,
signaling the arrival of another scrubbed angel
to see our adopted son through the night,
so we could sleep on the miniature pullout
behind the curtain in the corner, or try.
Did not expect the strip mall parking lot
rendezvous, pulling up beside some random
dude and his wife so she could unload her cooler
of frozen D.B.M. into the cooler in our trunk.
And now? Waking to sudden midnight cries
of a baby boy who looks nothing like me
or my wife, who looks nothing like me. I rise
to find his baby body free-falling in the bassinet,
hurtling through spacetime at 67,000 mph,
duly terrified. I rock him in the shadows
till he returns to a cocoon of amniotic dreams.
Morning next, after his bottle, we sprawl out
in daylight on the very solid living room rug,
studying the Other's smile, exchanging it.

William Shows Up

You will not remember how she cradled
you beneath the budding maple tree
your first week on Glendale Avenue. How
she turned her back on the horizon to keep
the day's sharp lastlight from waking you.

Yes, you will sleep for some time yet.
You will not remember the chickadees
in the bush nor the swell of the wind
nor the sound of your sister conjuring
things in the cut grass. I am writing to

remind you of that day she found a
castle in the front yard, and the wind
smelled like a glass of water, and there
were chickadees chattering in the bush.
She held you in the shade of the maple
tree like an antique vase, yet you were
astoundingly new and sound asleep.

Will you believe me? One day you may
think it a dream. Just remember: I was
there. I am writing to remind you that
you were too.

Amarillo Sepia

Would you look at the look on that kid,
balanced on a tree stump in his underwear

and a white cowboy hat, staring blankly
at the camera with both feet suspended
in the air like some precocious bull rider
awaiting his initiation to the Texas heat.

Look, too, at the young woman stooped
before him in the brittle grass with a towel,

soon to wipe the sand and creek water
from his soft feet: her swimsuit top and
denim shorts, her auburn hair braided
behind a white kerchief, her countenance

veiled by the shade of a cottonwood,
avoiding the photograph, looking off.

Moonhand

We stationed my new telescope on the tailgate
and took turns peering into insatiate reaches
of desert sky over Amarillo's outskirts, alight
like every other night. Gene focused the dial
on a marble moon, stepped back, and held
his hand five inches from the eyepiece,
catching out of the crisp air a pale bar of light.
Luminous nickel, vatic birthmark, magic
trick tattoo. Rusty motes of desert dust dancing
through the beam, the way snowflakes will
vie for the spotlight of any old street lamp.
Grinning, he slid his hand back into his pocket,
as if to hoodwink the very night. Morning
next it was everywhere and everywhere
at once—the far-flung shreds of the selfsame
sun, violet, aureate, red, flashing over
a fresh plain of hoarfrost atop earth's crust,
a day's worth of manna, already melting.
We took in what we could, then went for coffee.

Aubade

Black coffee cup on

                off-white kitchen table,

brimming, steaming

                in soft morning; sun

shafting through glass,

                casting shadows west on

off-white kitchen walls.

                Crescent halo of light

gleaming atop its oily umber

                face, glint of eye—

promising when full,

                promising when empty

to be fulfilled

                again.

Nocturne

Our words begin to atrophy
        beside the waning summer fire,
like sparks who would revise the stars

but fizzle out before they reach
        the canyon rim. Shadows descend
like geese upon a quiet lake,

or like a friend who need not speak
        to say, whose company is just
as sweet as solitude, or is

itself a kind of solitude.
        We watch a few last flames flicker
across the incandescent coals

until a virgin darkness drapes
        the woods, and day is reconciled
to night, and night to day, and the moon

emits its passive radiance
        that all should come to rest, and sleep
restore the fragile dreams of men.

Camp Judson

Then they worshiped in rapt adoration,
    encircling a roaring blaze ten feet tall
and wide, and the obsidian sky
    was slung with sparks soaring hot
with a hundred praises, heavenward,
    beyond the tops of the tallest pines.

Seething I slashed every last chord
    on my acoustic guitar like a madman
hacking logs, but their sound was drowned
    in the swell of voices, mellifluous voices.
And the faces lining the circle's rim
    were lit and lifted heavenward also,
    and several glistened with tears.

Three Ways of Looking at Spearfish

—Black Hills, South Dakota

I. Lookout Mountain

Just here the timbered foothills
of the northern Black Hills converge
on an unyielding
sweep of Wyoming prairie—

before which sits Spearfish,
pretty much a pit stop
along its slash of I-90, tiny
semis, cars, and Harleys
transporting travelers this way
and that, in what appears
from here—my lofty precipice
—like slow motion.

With enough distance, perhaps,
with enough elevation, I could
halt time altogether. I could
pray about everything
I've been meaning
to for some time.

II. Community Caves

Deep within the canyon now
a diaphanous waterfall dances
before the mouth of a cave
studded with variegated carabiners
of mountaineers gone by.
I lie alone in the cave's cool,

observing a red handprint
pressed against the brittle limestone,
work of a local art student
in some exalted state
of consciousness, no doubt, or
the burial site of Ezra Kind,
mythic Black Hills gold-rush brigand
who, two hundred summers ago, lost
everything in a barbarous treasure hunt.

We consider his fugitive days
on the frontier a cautionary tale
of avarice, forgetting that, long before
the lust of the flesh
or the lust of the eyes
or the pride of life
appeared

there was gold in the land of Havilah,
and the gold of that land was good.

But never mind Havilah.
I'm speaking of Spearfish—
noonday breeze honeyed with pine
sap supple amber sunlight
shattering the diaphanous waterfall
dancing before me and for me
the echoing cries of eagles
echoing through the canyon like
creatures freshly resurrected
—speaking of a land's primordial
claim to the heart of man.

III. Crow Peak

I remember when the mountain burned,
she said, a young waitress morena
at the Mexican restaurant.
*Lightning struck the mountain
and wildfires spread for many days,
feasting on wildflowers
and ponderosa deadfall
infested with pine beetles.
In daylight, it smoldered mutely
among the clouds. But at night,
at night the mountain glowed
blood-orange in the west,
ponderous as Cerberus crouching
at the dark rim of the planet…*

Anyway, she paused to count our change
and slid it across the counter, *hope
you enjoy the view.*

The view proved a dizzying expanse
of hazy blues and evergreens
drawing forever away from
the ashen soil beneath our throbbing boots.
Surveying that long country, my friend
with whom I'd shared the hike
uttered something profound,
I think, but can't remember what.
In truth, I hardly recognized a thing,
given the sudden shadow
of an unpropitious thunderhead
descending from the northwest.
Without another word, then, we tore

off our shirts and hurtled down
the mountainside as sparks of rain
stung our faces. We leapt over
toppled pines and lucid streams
like Prometheus fleeing the gods.
Between fierce peals of thunder
we shouted through mounting rain
of the love we owed our sublunary
lives and the songs we'd summon
from our guitars, if we ever made it home.

Late Aspiration

Not only possible but probable that
today's most needful determination lies
dormant among the caches of the past.
Not in novel resolve or chimerical re-
inventions of self, but words once pledged
to another (beloved because pledged-to)
in the crystal stillness of a winter
morning, in lucid lines laid down beside
the open window, buried in the file cabinet of

time: words ever-waiting for you to return
this day, to show them some late aspiration.

Acknowledgments

I'D LIKE TO THANK my professors and editors—Scott Cairns, Jennifer Maier, Mischa Willett, and D.S. Martin—for graciously tending to these poems.

To my poet-colleagues from Seattle Pacific University, thank you for your candor, humor, and charity. I still take heart when I think of you, out there, writing.

Thanks also to my church family at Grace PCA, particularly Mark Bertrand, whose counsel, encouragement, and writerly example underpin this little work.

Many thanks to my pencil pals at Blackwing; to Darin Kaihoi and the tireless baristas of Coffea Roasterie; and to the entire bearded staff at Last Stop CD Shop. Turns out writing a book is a rather material business.

More than a couple of these poems sprang from encounters with paintings by my good friend Zach Moll, to whom I owe a debt of gratitude (and probably a beer).

And to Jenny and Rudy—my love.

Finally, special thanks to the editors of the following publications, in which earlier versions of these poems first appeared:

"Early Morning Embers" in *Ad Fontes Journal*

"Nocturne" in *Cumberland River Review*

"Icarus Flashback" and "McKennan's Golden Hour" in *Ekstasis Magazine*

"Once Again, the Orchard" in *Eunoia Review*

"Camp Judson" and "The Centurion" in *Heart of Flesh Literary Journal*

"Telemachus" in *The Hyacinth Review*

"Poem from the Future" in *Inter-View*

"North Shore Vesper" in *Modern Reformation Magazine*

"Pickup Smells" in *New Verse Review*

"Post-blizzard" in *The North American Anglican*

"Red Light" in *North Dakota Quarterly*

Acknowledgments

"Forbearance"; "White Space"; and "The Handyman's Son" in *Pasque Petals*

"The Mower and the Nun" and "The End of Confession" in *Poetry East*

"East River, South Dakota" in *Reformed Journal*

"The Cottonwoods Were Sowing Starry Seeds" and "Driving at Night" in *The 2022 Scurfpea Publishing Poetry Anthology*

"The Seagull Scans a Fallow Field"; "Antique Store, Somewhere, South Dakota"; and "Prairie Archipelago" in *Solum Journal*

"When the Black Hills Are White" in *South Dakota Magazine*

The Poiema Poetry Series

COLLECTIONS IN THIS SERIES INCLUDE:

Six Sundays Toward a Seventh by Sydney Lea
Epitaphs for the Journey by Paul Mariani
Within This Tree of Bones by Robert Siegel
Particular Scandals by Julie L. Moore
Gold by Barbara Crooker
A Word In My Mouth by Robert Cording
Say This Prayer into the Past by Paul Willis
Scape by Luci Shaw
Conspiracy of Light by D.S. Martin
Second Sky by Tania Runyan
Remembering Jesus by John Leax
What Cannot Be Fixed by Jill Pelaez Baumgaertner
Still Working It Out by Brad Davis
The Hatching of the Heart by Margo Swiss
Collage of Seoul by Jae Newman
Twisted Shapes of Light by William Jolliff
These Intricacies by David Harrity
Where the Sky Opens by Laurie Klein
True, False, None of the Above by Marjorie Maddox
The Turning Aside anthology edited by D.S. Martin
Falter by Marjorie Stelmach
Phases by Mischa Willett
Second Bloom by Anya Krugovoy Silver
Adam, Eve, & the Riders of the Apocalypse anthology edited by D.S. Martin
Your Twenty-First Century Prayer Life by Nathaniel Lee Hansen
Habitation of Wonder by Abigail Carroll
Ampersand by D.S. Martin
Full Worm Moon by Julie L. Moore
Ash & Embers by James A. Zoller
The Book of Kells by Barbara Crooker
Reaching Forever by Philip C. Kolin
The Book of Bearings by Diane Glancy

In a Strange Land anthology edited by D.S. Martin
What I Have I Offer With Two Hands by Jacob Stratman
Slender Warble by Susan Cowger
Madonna, Complex by Jen Stewart Fueston
No Reason by Jack Stewart
Abundance by Andrew Lansdown
Angelicus by D.S. Martin
Trespassing on the Mount of Olives by Brad Davis
The Angel of Absolute Zero by Marjorie Stelmach
Duress by Karen An-hwei Lee
Wolf Intervals by Graham Hillard
To Heaven's Rim anthology edited by Burl Horniachek
Cup My Days Like Water by Abigail Carroll
Soon Done with the Crosses by Claude Wilkinson
House of 49 Doors by Laurie Klein
Hawk and Songbird by Susan Cowger
Ponds by J.C. Scharl
The Farewell Suites by Andrew Lansdown
Let's Call It Home by Luke Harvey

www.ingramcontent.com/pod-product-compliance
Lightning Source LLC
Chambersburg PA
CBHW022123040426
42450CB00006B/816